Contents

Reams of Wrapping

The Importance of Packaging

In America and Europe during the nineteenth century, people did their shopping at a general store. Dry goods, such as cereals, sugar and tea were individually weighed then packed in twists of paper and wrappings of the shopkeeper's own design.

The first mass-produced paper bags were made in Pennsylvania in 1852, but it was the production of the folding carton that revolutionized packaging. Cartons could be used to package a wide variety of products. Packaging soon became as important as the product itself.

Laundry basket made by Lois Walpole out of recycled apple juice cartons and cardboard.

The Purpose of Packaging

Packaging is a term used to describe a vast range of materials and containers. Its purpose is to protect and advertise the products we purchase in our shops. Packaging becomes worthless and disposable once its contents are used. Cardboard boxes, tubes, cans, plastic tapes and wires, cartons, bottle tops and labels are some of the items you can collect. They do have value and this book makes some exciting suggestions for putting to good use packaging that might once have been considered rubbish.

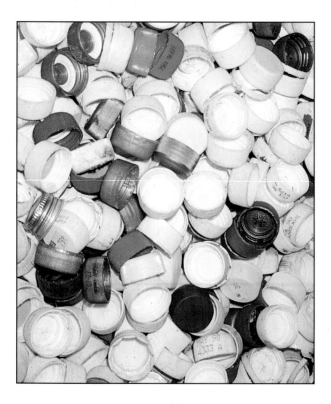

Plastic bottle tops can be used in a variety of art projects.

ART FROM PACKAGING

with projects using cardboard, plastics, foil and tape

Gillian Chapman & Pam Robson

HODDER
Wayland

Art from Fabric
Art from Packaging
Art from Paper
Art from Rocks and Shells
Art from Sand and Earth
Art from Wood

For more information on this series and other Hodder Wayland titles, go to www.hodderwayland.co.uk

This book was prepared for Wayland (Publishers) Ltd by Globe Education, Nantwich, Cheshire
Artwork and design by Gillian Chapman
Photography by Rupert Horrox

First published in 1996 by Wayland (Publishers) Ltd

This paperback edition published in 2005 by Hodder Wayland, an imprint of Hodder Children's Books

Printed in China

British Library Cataloguing in Publication Data
Chapman, Gillian
Art from Packaging. – (Salvaged series)
I. Title. II. Robson, Pam. III. Series
745.584

ISBN 0 7502 4782 7

Picture Acknowledgments
Ecoscene 4b (Sally Morgan), 5t (Whatmore)
Lois Walpole 4t, 5b

Hodder Children's Books
A division of Hodder Headline Limited
338 Euston Road, London NW1 3BH

Precycling

About 30 per cent of manufactured plastic is used for packaging; about half the weight of the plastic we throw away is packaging. One way to help avoid this waste is to precycle, which means to stop buying goods packaged in layers of unnecessary plastic wrappers. Buy drinks in glass bottles and aluminium cans that can be recycled.

Aluminium cans re-used as building material in Botswana, Africa.

Recycling Packaging

Aluminium cans are about 20 per cent cheaper to recycle than to make and need 5 per cent of the energy. In Padua a model of the Basilica Sant'Antonio has been erected using 3,250,000 cans, collected from streets and homes. In 1992, Sweden collected 787 million cans. How many can you collect and recycle?

During the Second World War (1939–1945), people were asked to salvage all useful items that might otherwise have been discarded. Rubbish was sorted into separate bins. Present day recycling points are organized in the same way. Scrap iron was claimed by the government for munitions, even iron railings were removed, and aluminium saucepans were turned into aeroplanes. Modern packagers can re-use aluminium, glass paper and card – make sure you sort your rubbish and take it to your local collection point.

A large dish made by Lois Walpole from used cans.

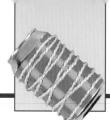

Printing Patterns

Printing Blocks

Printing blocks are traditionally made from wood; the harder the wood the more delicate the carving. These blocks interlock so that a repeating pattern can be accurately printed over a large area. Indian craftworkers are highly skilled at producing intricate designs printed on cotton textiles.

You can use a whole range of packaging materials to make exciting patterns. Simple printing blocks can be made from polystyrene packing. The blocks are easy to carve and shape, yet are firm enough to use many times.

Prints made with Packaging

Textured Prints

To make a textured print, find a large piece of textured wrapping such as bubblewrap or corrugated card. Cover this with coloured ink or paint and press gently on to a piece of plain paper. Leave it to dry, then carefully peel off the wrapping. It will have left a colourful, textured pattern.

This kind of print is called a monoprint. The wrapping cannot be used again in the same way, which makes every print unique. With repeated printing methods, each print made from the same block is identical and prints can be made until the block wears out.

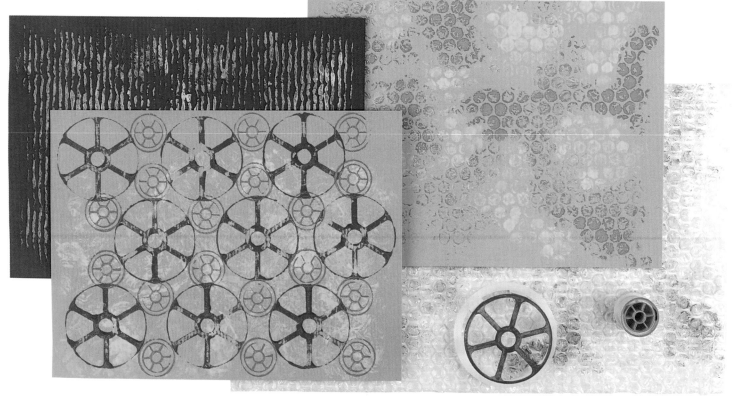
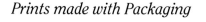

Repeating Patterns

Many items of packaging make ideal printing tools. Plastic spools and lids come in a variety of interesting shapes and sizes. See what you can find and experiment with different types. Use them to print repeating patterns and designs over the textured prints.

Printing Cans

Another way of making a repeating print involves using an empty drink can. Wind lengths of string around the can to make a pattern, and tie the string firmly in place. Cover the can in paint so that the string picks up all the colour. Then slowly roll it over a strip of paper. You can see the results in the examples shown here.

Cover can with paint.

Print stripes.

Printing Cans

Packaging Prints

Printed Gift wrap

It is now common for gift wrap and greetings cards to be printed on recycled paper. By printing your own papers you are being environmentally aware and avoiding further waste. You can produce unusual designs for special occasions.

Printed Pictures

A portfolio is a useful storage container for your prints. They can also be displayed in frames made from recycled materials. In this way you create a complete 'salvaged' work of art.

Finished Portfolio

Place strong tape diagonally across the corners of the portfolio covers.

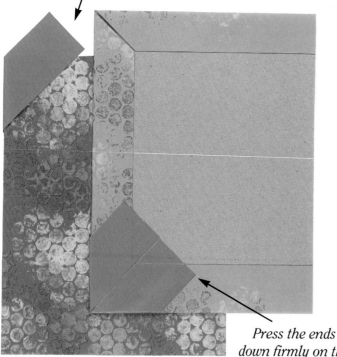

Press the ends down firmly on the back of the card.

Taping the Corners of the Portfolio

Making a Portfolio

The size of the portfolio you make will depend upon the size of your artwork. The measurements given here are for a portfolio designed to store A2 prints.

Cut two large pieces of scrap card 65 centimetres by 45 centimetres. Cover the outside of the card using your own printed papers, taping across the corners for extra protection. Cover the inside of both cards, again using printed papers.

Tape the covers together along the longest sides. Make flaps to fit inside one of the covers and glue them in place to hold the artwork. Cut slots in the two covers and thread tape through to fasten the portfolio.

Picture Frames

To make a frame to fit a particular piece of artwork you will need to work to precise measurements. Cut a frame from stiff card, making the window opening 2 centimetres smaller than the print. The width of the frame should be 6 centimetres all round. Make a backing card the same size as the frame.

The frames shown here have been covered with squares of corrugated card, crumpled foil and coloured twine. Decorate the frame and paint it first before attaching the backing card. Finally mount your print between them. Glue a strip of card to the back of the frame to give it support.

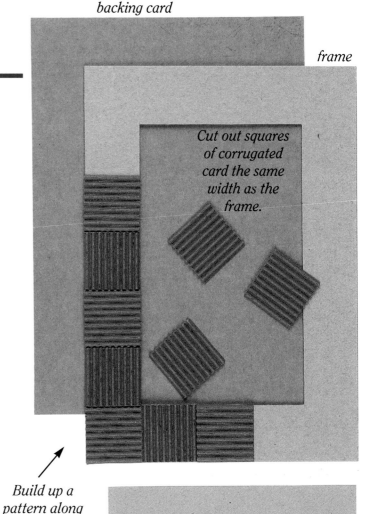

backing card

frame

Cut out squares of corrugated card the same width as the frame.

Build up a pattern along the frame.

Making Picture Frames

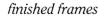

finished frames

back view

Plastic Art

Plastics

Some plastics are biodegradable, most are not. It is possible to melt down certain plastic items for re-use in another form. The rest must be burned, causing toxic fumes, or tipped into landfall sites, creating methane gas which can be dangerous. Soft-drink bottles made from polyethylene terephthalate (PET) can be melted down and turned into a cottony fibre. This can be used as insulation or even for new carpets.

Plastic Products

Look around you and see how much plastic has been used and discarded. Start to make a plastic collection which can be used for project work. Plastic bags and wrappings, tapes and twines are perfect for craftwork – the more colourful they are, the better.

Woven Mats

Colourful mats can be made from different types of plastic tapes and twine woven and twisted around card shapes. Cut out the mat shape from a piece of scrap card and make notches along the two opposite sides. Wind thin flexible plastic twine or wire around the notches, as shown here. Then weave across the twine with thicker tapes. The finished mats are both attractive and practical.

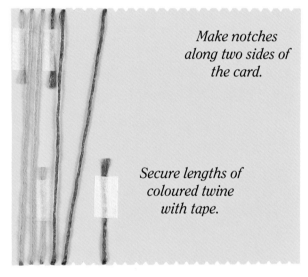

Make notches along two sides of the card.

Secure lengths of coloured twine with tape.

making the frame

finished mat

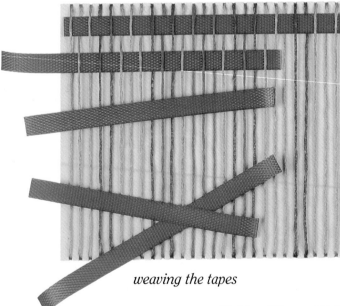

weaving the tapes

Making Woven Mats

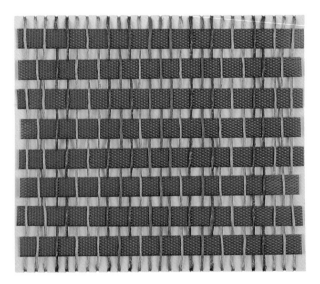

Purposeful Projects

In the 1950s, the mass-production of flexible plastic made it ideal for packaging. It was hygienic, cheap and malleable. Until recently, manufacturers used it without any thought for the environmental consequences.

By using non-recyclable packaging for purposeful projects you can make a positive contribution towards reducing the size of the rubbish mountains, and help conserve Earth's natural resources.

Plastic Picture

Plastic Twine and Packaging

Plastic Pictures

Weaving a picture out of plastic materials makes use of a wide range of disposable packaging. First you will need to draw a simple picture on paper, then place a piece of plastic netting over the top. Weave different coloured lengths of plastic in and out of the netting, following the design behind the mesh. Choose colours and textures that suit the subject. Mount the finished picture on to a plastic backing.

Woven Baskets

Natural Baskets

Palm fronds were the first fans. Whole leaves were the first umbrellas. The first baskets were woven using readily available natural materials, usually rattans. Baskets can be made by weaving or coiling. Werregue baskets, made by the Waunana people of Columbia, were so tightly coiled and stitched that water could be carried in them. Today the Waunana use plastic to make their baskets, while the original baskets fetch high prices amongst collectors.

Modern Baskets

Basketmakers like Lois Walpole, who live and work in an urban environment, have developed the art of weaving using modern packaging materials. Cardboard, netting and plastic are woven into colourful, practical baskets using traditional methods. Here are two baskets you can make using modern materials.

Banana-Shaped Basket

This simple basket is made from 6 strips of strong cardboard 3 centimetres by 30 centimetres. Paint the card first using bright PVA paints and let it dry before cutting. Then punch holes in the strips, 3 centimetres from each end. Assemble the strips and fasten them at one end with a large paper fastener. Fan out the basket and weave coloured twine in and out of the strips before fastening the other end.

strips attached with one fastener

basket shape formed with two fasteners

Loosely weave twine in between the strips before securing the second fastener.

Assemble basket and tighten the twine to keep the shape.

Making a Banana-Shaped Basket

Woven Plate

To make the plate, find some cardboard that is both strong and flexible. Paint it with PVA colours and cut it into 3 centimetre by 30 centimetre strips. Weave the strips together, as shown here, holding them in place with pegs.

When the weaving is the correct shape and size, trim off any surplus lengths of card. Staple the woven strips in position. Measure around the edge of the plate and cut an 8 centimetre card strip to the same length. Fold this in half length-ways and bind it around the edge, holding it in place with pegs. Sew this strip to the plate using coloured wire or twine with a blunt-ended needle.

Making a Woven Plate

weaving the strips

adding the binding

Finished Plates and Basket

Woven Boxes

Cardboard Cities

In some parts of the world, there are shanty towns built on the edges of large cities. Here poor people use materials, like cardboard, that many would call waste. In other places, the homeless sleep under bridges and in doorways protected by cardboard boxes. The insulating properties of the cardboard help to keep these people warm.

Cardboard Boxes

The production of a cardboard box that could be folded from one piece of flat card revolutionized packaging in the 1850s. Cartons became cheap and easy to produce, but were also disposable. Modern society has become dependent on the cardboard box to package almost everything we buy.

Look at the cartons and boxes used in shops and supermarkets to package food products, toiletries and many other items. Many have interesting graphics and labelling. A great deal of time and money goes into their design, yet they are rarely re-used and most of them are thrown away.

Three-Dimensional Weaving

A cardboard box can be used again as a structure for a three-dimensional weaving. Find a suitable box and seal the top and bottom with tape. Paint all the sides to cover up any printing and cut a series of notches in the edges. Wind coloured plastic twine around these notches. Further twine and tape can then be interwoven, forming a three-dimensional woven cube.

Painted Box with Weaving

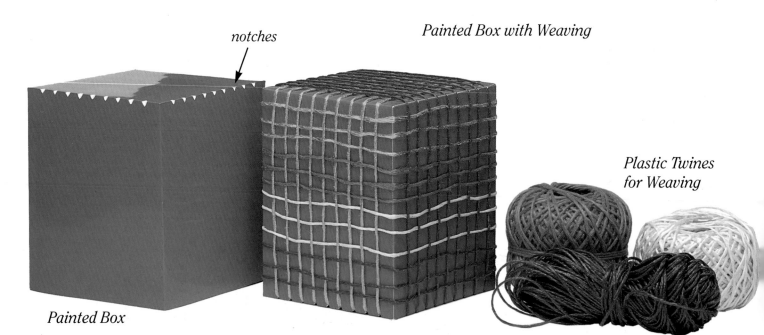

notches

Painted Box

Plastic Twines for Weaving

Woven Boxes

These boxes are woven from strips of flexible cardboard. Use any scrap card – cereal boxes arc ideal – painting them first to disguise any printed surface.

Cut ten card strips 3 centimetres by 45 centimetres and weave them into place as shown, forming the base of the box. Bend each card strip so it forms a right angle to the base. Cut five strips 3 centimetres by 70 centimetres and weave them through these strips, forming the sides of the box. Finish off by tucking the ends inside the box.

Finishing Off

Cut a strip of card 6 centimetres by 65 centimetres and crease it along the centre. Fold it over the top edge of the box. Sew the strip into place with coloured twine, using a large blunt-ended needle and blanket stitch. To make a lid use ten card strips 3 centimetres by 24 centimetres and follow the weaving instructions for the box.

Weaving a Box

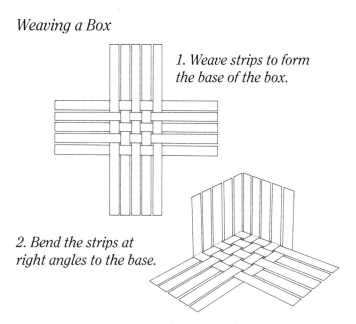

1. Weave strips to form the base of the box.

2. Bend the strips at right angles to the base.

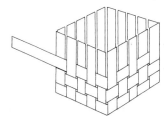

3. Weave strips around the box to form the sides.

Finished Woven Box and Lid

15

Figures from Foil

Packaging with Foil

Between 1910 and 1920, two new materials were introduced to the packaging industry. They were aluminium foil and Cellophane. They were used to wrap many different products, especially food, keeping it clean and fresh. Because it is such a practical material, aluminium is used extensively today to package a great variety of foods, from fresh and frozen items to fizzy drinks.

Aluminium is an attractive material for packaging because it is lightweight and malleable. It is also an easy material to recycle. Seattle, USA, has introduced a recycling programme that recovers 45 per cent of its waste. From 1·7 million tonnes of aluminium thrown away in a year, 1 million tonnes are recycled. Cans are 20 per cent cheaper to make from recycled aluminium, and the process requires only 5 per cent of the energy.

Working with Foil

Foil is a soft material and so it is easy to shape. Collect together some discarded foil containers, such as plates or small pie dishes; make sure they are cleaned thoroughly before using them. Foil can be cut with scissors, but be careful of any sharp edges.

Making Foil Figures

Find several clean, foil plates of different shapes and sizes. A large round plate can make the base for a foil figure. Draw patterns on to the foil with a ball-point pen. The pen will leave impressions in the soft foil. Cut out sections and shapes from the smaller plates for features and staple them to the base. Finally cut a slot in the base of a small foil dish and use it as a stand for the foil figure.

Foil Figure

Making a Foil Hanging

To make a foil picture first cut a base out of thin card, about 30 centimetres square. Cut a piece of foil, about 5 centimetres larger than the card. Crinkle the foil and then carefully flatten it. Using PVA, glue it to the card, overlapping the sides as shown here.

Find a clean foil plate which is about 20 centimetres in diameter. Draw a face design on the plate, using a ball-point pen to make patterns. Cut out the eyes and mouth with scissors. Glue the face to the foil backing.

Making a Foil Face

Covering Card with Foil

Colouring Foil

To give the background foil a burnished, metallic look, try painting it with coloured ink. Be careful not to flatten the crinkled texture. Tape two ring-pull tabs to the back of the picture and use them to pin it to the wall.

Junk Art

Found Objects

Artists are often inspired by the shape of a particular object when creating a work of art. Picasso used a toy car to shape the head on his baboon sculpture. He created many sculptures out of found objects and then cast them in bronze. He also made a bull's head out of a bicycle saddle and a pair of handlebars.

Junk Figures

A Second Chance

Unnecessary packaging adds to the mountains of rubbish accumulating in our throw-away world. Products are packaged in many ways, but paper containers coated with wax or lined with plastic cannot be recycled. It is these items that we need to re-use.

Give all packaging a second chance. Can an empty container or bottle be used again in a practical way, or does it suggest to you a particular figure or shape? You may be able to use it in a fun way. Look at the ideas here and try to think up some of your own.

Junk Figures

These figures have been made from a range of plastic bottles and containers. Paint the containers first with acrylic paints and then glue scraps of coloured paper, tape and fabric to them. Half fill them with sand or gravel and use them as skittles.

Tubular Figures

Cardboard tubes and rolls are very strong structures that are used to support many household products. Here is a way to put them to good use.

Collect together a selection of different sized tubes. Large tubes will be needed for the head and body, with smaller diameter tubes for the neck, arms and legs. Paint the tubes or cover them in coloured wrapping paper before assembling the figures.

Using a large needle, make holes in the tubes, as shown in the diagram. Then thread stiff wire through the holes to make the joints, securing each end with a loop.

Different Cardboard Tubes

Making Tubular Figures

Thread stiff wire through holes to make joints.

Attach card hands and feet to the figures.

19

Plant Pots

Make drainage holes in plastic containers.

Growing

Propagating flowers and vegetables from seeds or cuttings makes a very purposeful and satisfying occupation. Plastic containers are ideal to use as plant pots and are now widely used by gardeners as a cheaper alternative to terracotta. All the containers you need for growing seeds and rooting cuttings can be recycled from everyday household containers.

Choosing Containers

Plastic yoghurt pots, ice-cream and margarine containers can all be used as plant pots for young seedlings. Larger plastic or foil food trays are ideal for sowing small seeds. However, all these containers must be thoroughly washed before re-using, and if plants are to grow, the containers must have adequate drainage holes.

Collect suitable containers and seeds. If you do not have a garden you can grow seeds successfully on a window ledge. It is also easy to propagate house plants from cuttings. Keep a record of their growth in a journal.

Seedlings and Cuttings Growing in Plastic Containers

Notebook to Record Plant Growth

26th April
Planted cuttings —
Spider plant, cactus
σ succulents

Seedlings —
Mustard σ cress
1cm tall.

Woven Pots

Decorated Pots

Decorating Pots

Containers can be used just as they are once they have been washed. However you can make them more decorative. Cut an odd number of slits in the sides and weave lengths of coloured tapes in and out, or cover them with coloured plastic twine. Attach the twine to the pots with strips of double-sided Sellotape.

Bottle Gardens

Plants growing in a bottle create their own ecosystem and once watered, will need very little attention. You will need a large, clear, bottle, a disused storage jar is ideal. Put a 4 centimetre layer of gravel in the bottom of the jar, with a 10 centimetre layer of soil on top. Find out which plants grow well in a damp atmosphere and plant them in the bottle. When you next use disposable plastic cutlery, take it home and wash it. It makes ideal tools for pot gardening. Use a plastic bottle as a watering-can.

Bottle Garden

Bottle Garden Tools

Musical Junk

Early Instruments

The first musical instruments were made from natural materials – the resonance of wood makes it an ideal material for drums. Seeds inside gourds make rattles and shakers. People have always used whatever materials were at hand to make music. You can create a whole orchestra of sounds by using packaging and junk materials that might otherwise be thrown away.

Many of the instruments featured on this page have their origins in the distant past. Music has always been a source of pleasure, as well as an important means of communication. Much African music is based on speech. The pitch of African 'talking' drums imitates the natural sounds of the language.

Junk Drums and Shakers

Experiment with a selection of plastic, tin and cardboard containers. Each will give a different sound if struck like a drum. If the same containers are filled with dry materials like seeds or sand, you will hear a whole range of new sounds when you shake them. To make a drum, cut the end off a large balloon and stretch it over the open container, taping it firmly in place. Decorate the drums and shakers with coloured card, tape and stickers.

Dried Materials for Shakers

Container Drums

Shakers

Decorate drums and shakers with coloured card, tape and stickers.

Bottle top Castanets

Rattles, Tambourines and Castanets

Rattles are the simplest musical instrument and are found world-wide. In Kenya, rattles like the one shown here, are made from bottle tops threaded on to a wire loop. Castanets and tambourines are favourite instruments to accompany dancers. Metal or plastic lids attached to flexible card make excellent castanets. The tambourine is made from two foil dishes stapled together and decorated with ribbons and bells.

Plastic Didgeridoo

The didgeridoo is a traditional Aboriginal instrument. It is used in rituals to communicate with ancestors. This music is a series of almost continuous notes. Aboriginal musicians have developed the special breathing skills needed to make the familiar sounds. This didgeridoo is made from a one metre length of plastic or cardboard tubing and it will amplify humming sounds.

Bottle Top Rattle

Tambourine

Didgeridoo

Decorate with coloured tape and stickers.

Puppets from Packaging

Shadow Puppets

The first puppets were made in Asia, where they were used to bring to life ancient myths and legends. Cambodia, Thailand, Malaysia and Bali have long-established shadow puppet traditions. The grotesquely fantastic shadow puppets of Java are perhaps the most splendid. Jointed puppets are manipulated by a series of long rods which keep the shadow of the puppetmaster away from the performance.

Making the Theatre

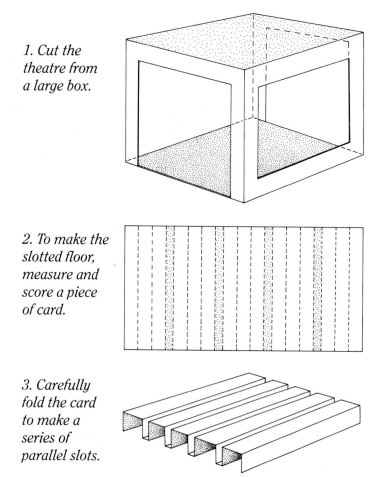

1. Cut the theatre from a large box.

2. To make the slotted floor, measure and score a piece of card.

3. Carefully fold the card to make a series of parallel slots.

Collecting Materials

It is a simple matter to set up a theatre and make puppets. The main material you need is plenty of scrap cardboard of different thicknesses. The theatre is made from a large, strong cardboard box, the scenery and puppets are made from thinner card that can be painted.

Planning the Story-Line

Before you make the puppets and design the scenery you will need to decide on a story-line for a play. Write an outline keeping your ideas very simple. Two scenes and four characters will be sufficient. You can only operate two puppets at a time single-handed.

Making the Theatre

Cut the front and sides out of a large cardboard box, as shown here. The puppets slide along in slots in the stage floor. To make the floor find a piece of thin card and cut it to the same width as the theatre. Score and fold the card as shown, making a series of parallel slots in the card. Make sure the wooden dowels that are attached to the puppets fit into the slots and move freely.

Finally paint the theatre and decorate it with coloured paper scraps or wrapping paper.

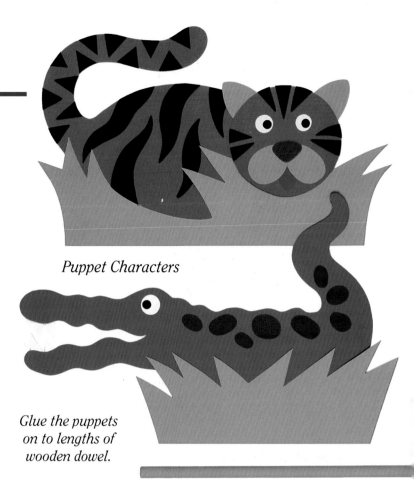

Puppet Characters

Sketch the puppet shapes on paper before drawing them on to card. These puppets are always seen in profile, so make sure that some of your characters are designed to enter from the left and others from the right.

Paint the puppets, cut them out and then glue them on to lengths of wooden dowel. Make pieces of scenery from card and position them in the slots.

Puppet Characters

Glue the puppets on to lengths of wooden dowel.

The Puppet Theatre

Make sure the wooden rods slide freely in the slots.

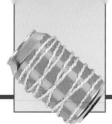

Junk Toys

Children at Play

Toys made from salvaged objects and materials are familiar in Africa today. In Botswana, they are now produced for export. Often the name of the original manufacturer is still visible on the finished toy, strangely this adds to the value. There are many African children who make toys from discarded objects because no other toys are available. In Kenya footballs are sometimes made out of plastic bags bound into a ball shape with string.

Automatons

Jointed toys became popular in Europe during the eighteenth century. By the nineteenth century they had become more complicated and were operated in a number of ways. The coiled spring was the most common method used. When the nineteenth century came to an end, the mass-produced, tin-plate toy industry was underway. Moving toys have been popular with children ever since. The majority of today's toys are made from plastic and are battery-powered.

Robot Automaton

This simple moving toy is made up of various shapes cut from plastic scraps. A popper fastened at each joint allows it to move freely. Use plastic that is rigid, yet thin enough for holes to be punched through to make the joints.

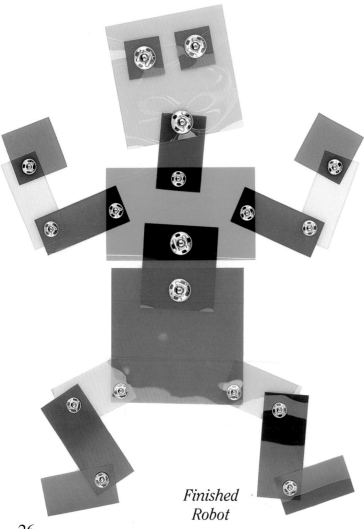

Finished Robot

Punch holes in plastic pieces.

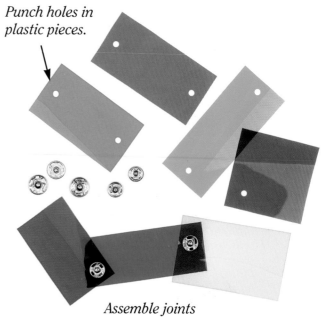

Assemble joints with large poppers.

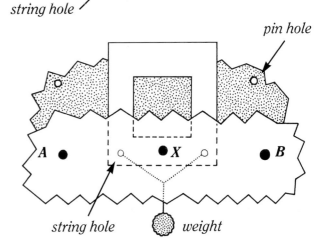

foreground

pin hole

head

background

string hole

A *X* *B*

Munching Rubbish

This toy is slightly more complicated and moves on a pivot, called the fulcrum. Cut the main pieces from strong, scrap card. Paint or cover them with a collage of paper, foil and plastic scraps. Make holes in the pieces, as shown.

Fix a weight to the head with two lengths of string. Attach the head to the background at point X using a split pin, making sure it moves freely. Assemble the foreground and background pieces at points A and B, using split pins. Pin the 'rubbish dump' to a wall, swing the weight and see the robot munch away.

pin hole

A *X* *B*

string hole *weight*

Assembling the Rubbish Dump Monster

Rubbish Dump Monster

swinging weight

Moving Wheels

Moving Around

You can create movement by building a system of interlocking cogs and wheels out of salvaged materials. Movement is transferred from one part of the machine to the next. A small cog interlocking with a large cog turns more frequently. These wheels do not move along, they simply turn round and round. Cog wheels can be seen inside old, mechanical clocks and watches.

Cogs and Wheels from Junk

Collect together a variety of circular junk items, such as shallow cheese containers and lids of different sizes. Glue lengths of lollipop sticks to each cog as shown here. Make a hole through the centre of each cog, then attach them to a card base. Make sure the cogs rotate freely and the spokes interlock. When one cog is turned all the others should move as well.

Moving Cogs and Wheels

Making the cogs.

Glue sticks firmly to lid.

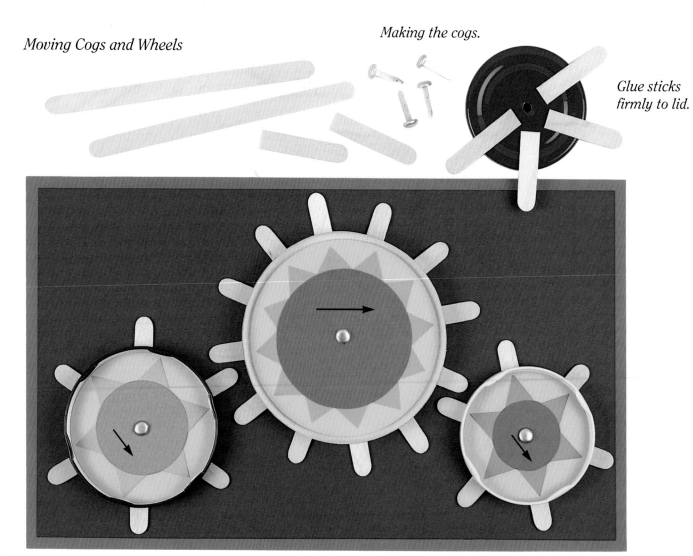

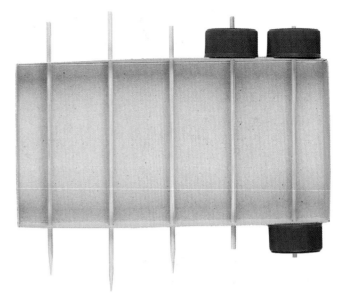

Moving Along

Here is an idea for making a three-dimensional machine that will move along a surface when pushed or pulled. This time you will need to collect together an even number of small plastic lids that are all the same size.

Making a Rolling Bug

Find or make a long, narrow box about 20 centimetres by 10 centimetres by 3 centimetres in size. Make a series of small holes along each side of the box – one hole for each pair of wheels. Use wooden kebab sticks for axles and thread them through the holes.

Assembling the Wheels and Axles

Make a hole in the centre of each lid. Push them on to the axle, cutting off any extra length. Secure each lid to its axle with a blob of glue. Attach a length of string to the front of the box to pull it along. Make sure it moves smoothly on the wheels.

Decorate the box with scraps of plastic, coloured paper and yarn, and turn it into a rolling bug.

Rolling Bug

Glossary

Aborigines An ancient people who lived in Australia long before it was discovered by Europeans.

automaton A machine that operates automatically.

axle A bar or shaft connecting the wheels on a vehicle.

biodegradable A material that decomposes naturally.

cuttings Small sections cut from plant stems that form their own roots in water or soil.

dowel A small length of wood used to join two other pieces of wood together.

ecosystem The interaction between living things within their environment.

fulcrum The pivot about which a lever turns.

gourds Fruit of plants of the cucumber family. In Africa, dried shells were often used to make musical instruments and other artefacts.

graphics The art of drawing to mathematical principles.

gravel A mixture of rock fragments and pebbles.

humid A moist, damp atmosphere.

journal A written daily record in book form.

junk Discarded objects.

labelling Paper, card or another material attached to an object in order to identify it.

landfill sites Large pits that are filled with alternate layers of rubbish and earth.

methane gas A colourless, odourless and flammable gas which can be used as a fuel.

monoprint A repeating pattern created with a unique printing block.

packaging Wrappings and boxes made specially to hold and protect retail items.

Picasso, Pablo Ruiz (1881-1973) A Spanish artist who is looked on by many people as the most inventive and innovative artist of the twentieth century.

portfolio A flat case used to store and carry papers.

propagate To grow new plants and cuttings.

rattans The stems of a climbing palm used for wickerwork and canes.

seedlings Young plants grown from seed.

shanty town Part of a town or city where very poor people live in ramshackle huts, often built from discarded materials.

More Information

Books to Read

Allen, Judy and Brown, Martin, *The Last Green Book on Earth*, Red Fox, 1994

Carlson, Laurie, *Ecoart!*, Williamson Publishing, 1992

Herald, Jacqueline, *World Crafts*, Lark Books, 1993

Terzian, Alexandra, *The Kids' Multicultural Art Book*, Williamson Publishing, 1993

Addresses for Information

Australia

Australian Conservation Foundation,
Floor 1, 60 Leicester Street, Carlton, Vic 3053

Canada

International Council for Local Environmental Initiatives, City Hall, East Tower, 8th Floor, Toronto, Ontario M5H 2N2

UK

British Plastics Federation, 6 Bath Place, Rivington Street, London EC2A 3JE

Recoup, Metro Centre, Welbeck Way, Woodston, Peterborough PE2 7UH

Places to Visit (UK)

Children's Scrap Project, 137 Homerton High Street, Hackney, London E9 6AS

Commonwealth Institute, Kensington High Street, London W8 6NQ

Livesey Museum, 682 Old Kent Road, London SE15 1JF

Places to Visit (UK)

Children's Scrap Project, 137 Homerton High Street, Hackney, London E9

Commonwealth Institute, Kensington High Street, London W8 6NQ

Kids' Scrapbank, Shakespeare Avenue, London NW10

Livesey Museum, 682 Old Kent Road, London SE15 1JF

Museum of the Pack Age, Gloucester Docks, Gloucester

Art and Craft
1. Artists/Picasso
2. Environmental art/using recycled materials for printing/sculpture/models/weaving/puppets/picture frames/portfolios/collage

Mathematics
1. Nets and solid shapes
2. Two- and three-dimensional shapes

Music
1. Musical instruments
2. Musical jingles and advertisements

Design and Technology
1. Structures/joining materials/designing and making containers
2. Joints and levers/moving toys/wheels and axles

Topic Web Art from Packaging

Geography
1. Economic geography/world trade/import/export/tourism
2. Social geography/developing countries/ recycling packaging to make artefacts e.g. Botswana's toy industry
3. Environmental geography/changes caused by human development/landfill sites

Language and Literature
1. Rhyming jingles, advertisements/slogans
2. Drama scripts for puppet plays/puppet performances

History
1. Population growth/Industrial Revolution/market for mass-produced goods
2. History of retailing/mass production/packaging
3. Development of the railways/transporting bulk goods
4. The media/reaching the masses/growth of advertising

Science
1. Transferring energy/cogs and wheels
2. Properties of materials
3. Natural history/seeds and reproduction in plants
4. Ecosystems and pollution/habitats

Index